Thanksgiving Fun

Messner Holiday Library
Thanksgiving Fun
by Judith Hoffman Corwin

Julian Messner

Published by Julian Messner,
a division of Simon & Schuster,
Simon & Schuster Building, Rockefeller Center,
1230 Avenue of the Americas,
New York, New York 10020
Julian Messner and colophon are registered
trademarks of Simon & Schuster.
Manufactured in the United States of America

10 9 8 7 6 5 4 3 2 1 (hardcover)

10 9 8 7 6   (paperback)

Design by Judith Hoffman Corwin
Also available in Julian Messner Library Edition.
Library of Congress Cataloging in Publication Data.
Corwin, Judith Hoffman.
    Thanksgiving fun.

    (Messner holiday library)
    Includes index.
    Summary: Includes recipes for a traditional Thanks-
giving dinner as well as instructions for making a
Thanksgiving centerpiece, placemats, invitations, and
other seasonal craft projects.
    1. Thanksgiving decorations—Juvenile literature.
2. Handicraft—Juvenile literature. 3. Thanksgiving
cookery—Juvenile literature. [1. Thanksgiving decorations. 2. Thanksgiving cookery. 3. Handicraft.
4. Cookery, American] I. Title. II. Series.
TT900.T5C67   1984   745.597′1   83-25062
ISBN 0-671-49422-8
ISBN 0-671-50849-0 pbk.

For the illuminating leaves and starry nights of Autumn
and Jules Arthur and Oliver Jamie who share them with me.

MESSNER BOOKS BY JUDITH HOFFMAN CORWIN

Messner Holiday Library: Thanksgiving Fun
Messner Holiday Library: Halloween Fun
Messner Holiday Library: Christmas Fun
Messner Holiday Library: Valentine Fun

Contents

For You   8

Before You Begin   9

About Thanksgiving   10

Thanksgiving Dinner Menu   12

Recipes   13-21

Mayflower Thanksgiving Dinner Invitation   22

Gobble, Gobble Turkey Centerpiece   24

Tom Turkey Table Toppers   28

Autumn Leaves   32

Wilson and Wilhelmina Mouse   34

Sylvan Squirrel   38

Pilgrim and Native American Paper Puppets   40

Michael Moose Puppet   42

Native American Soap Charm   44

"Deerskin" Story Cloth   46

Calendar   48

Start a Mini Garden at Thanksgiving   61

Index   64

For You

Thanksgiving Fun will help to make this a holiday to remember. It is full of ideas for creating puppets, charms, decorations, presents, and even a delicious Thanksgiving dinner, from the invitation to the dessert. You will be able to make everything yourself, using mostly things that you can find around the house. You will also learn why we do some of the things we do on Thanksgiving.

Before You Begin

Make your own pattern

Directions for most of the projects in this book include patterns for you to make an exact copy of what is shown. You don't want to cut up the book, so make your own patterns with tracing paper. Begin by placing a piece of tracing paper over the pattern to be transferred from the book. Using a pencil with soft lead, trace over the outline of what is in the book. When you have finished, cut out what you have drawn on the tracing paper. Now you have your own pattern.

Using your pattern

Pin your pattern, tape it, or hold it down carefully on the paper or fabric you have chosen to work with. Draw around the edges of the pattern. Lift up the tracing paper pattern and go on with the other instructions for your project.

Materials you will need

The basic materials you need are readily available from stationery stores and art supply shops: cardboard, oaktag, heavy white paper, and colored paper. Extras like cloth and bits of lace may be found at home or at fabric departments in stores. For details or accents you'll need colored markers (waterproof), pencils, or watercolors. You will also need a sharp pair of scissors and a good brand of white glue.

Preparing a work area

Before starting to work, make sure that all your supplies are at hand and that everything is neat and clean. Cover your work surface with newspaper to protect it from glue. By the way, when you work with glue always spread a thin, even coat. A thin coat sticks better and is less likely to cause the paper to buckle.

Most projects in **Thanksgiving Fun** can be made quite easily. Some may prove more of a challenge—but you can do them all. Have fun!

About Thanksgiving

A thanksgiving festival at harvest time is an ancient custom. The Hebrews celebrated at a special eight-day feast. The ancient Greeks held a nine-day feast dedicated to Demeter, the goddess of agriculture. The pre-Christian Druid priests of Britain held a "harvest home" celebration, a feast after the last crops were reaped and stored for the long winter months ahead.

Our American Thanksgiving was first celebrated in 1621 at the Plymouth Colony in Massachusetts. Governor William Bradford ordered a day of Thanksgiving for surviving the very hard times the new settlers had gone through. All the colonists and the native Americans who lived nearby shared this great feast together. The natives had helped the colonists to survive, showing them new and wonderful foods so they wouldn't starve. The Indians taught the settlers to gather cranberries, to plant corn, to hunt wild turkeys, and to dig for clams.

After the American Revolution, President George Washington proclaimed the first national Thanksgiving Day to honor the adoption of the United States Constitution. This first American Thanksgiving was held on November 26, 1789. After that, days of thanksgiving were held in various parts of our country at different times. After the victory at Gettysburg in 1863, Abraham Lincoln named the last Thursday in November as Thanksgiving Day. However, Thanksgiving was not fully established as a *national* holiday. Each state decided when its Thanksgiving Day would be held. Finally, in 1941, when Franklin D. Roosevelt was President, Congress passed a special resolution declaring that Thanksgiving be celebrated on the fourth Thursday of November.

Thanksgiving is a special time to get together with family and good friends. We live in such exciting times it is often easy to forget our country's humble beginnings and the struggles which have made us great. Now we take a day to sit back and think about this year and past years, to say "thank you" and to celebrate our good fortune with a wonderful feast and a happy time!

The very best part of Thanksgiving is the wonderful, warm, cozy feeling of having the people we care about together on that day, relaxing and enjoying each other's company. And the next best things are the wonderful smells that come from the kitchen and the table set for good eating.

This is going to be a super special Thanksgiving feast because *you* are going to be doing the cooking—with a little adult supervision. The menu is traditional, but with a few different touches, like an English dessert. The dinner is easy to prepare and you can serve it with great pride. Remember to clean up the kitchen as you go along. The desserts, cranberry sauce, and bread can be made the day before so that you won't have so much to do on Thanksgiving itself.

Thanksgiving Dinner Menu

(This dinner will serve 6 to 8 people.)

Raw vegetables with sour cream and onion dip
Roast turkey
Fresh cranberry sauce with oranges
Stuffing with raisins
Molasses bread
Baked sweet potatoes with peaches
Cranberry and ginger ale punch
English trifle
Butter cookies

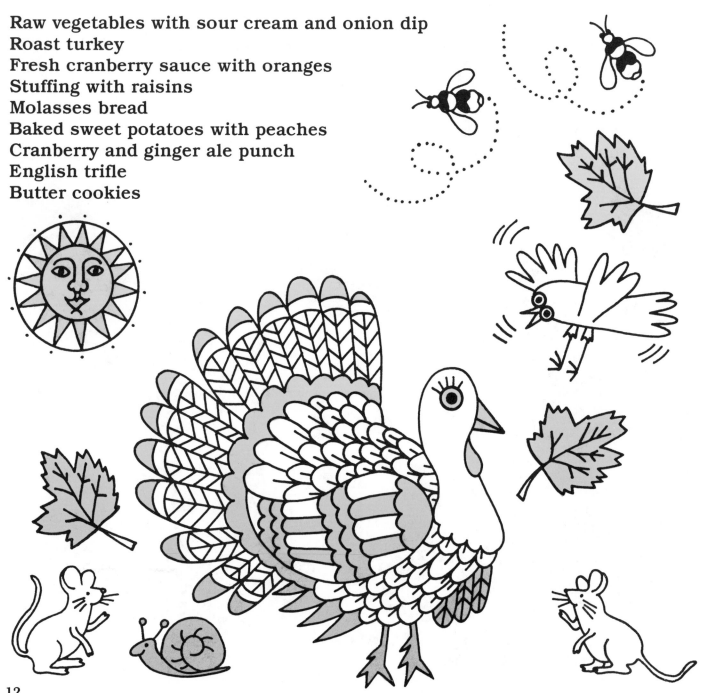

Raw Vegetables with Sour Cream and Onion Dip

Good and easy!

INGREDIENTS YOU WILL NEED:

Dip:

    2 cups sour cream
    1 envelope of dry onion soup mix
    1/4 teaspoon paprika

Vegetables (as many as you wish):

    thin asparagus
    broccoli
    carrot sticks (peeled and sliced into strips)
    cauliflower
    zucchini
    red and green peppers
    cucumber slices (peel the cucumber first)
    scallions (with green tops cut off)
    black and green olives
    cherry tomatoes

UTENSILS YOU WILL NEED:

mixing bowl
measuring cups and spoons
mixing spoon
serving platter and bowl

DIRECTIONS:

1. To make the dip, combine the soup mix, sour cream, and paprika. Put into a pretty bowl to serve from.
2. Wash and cut vegetables into bite-size pieces.
3. Arrange vegetables on a large platter. Place bowl with dip in the center of the platter.
4. Refrigerate.

Roast Turkey

This is what Thanksgiving is all about! Even though it takes a long time to cook, turkey is really simple to prepare.

INGREDIENTS YOU WILL NEED:

10 lb. turkey
2 tablespoons salt
2 tablespoons garlic powder
1/4 cup vegetable oil
1/4 cup bottled lemon juice
8 carrots (peeled and sliced)
2 medium-sized onions (peeled and sliced)
2 cups tomato sauce
2 cups cold water
1 cup apricot jam

UTENSILS YOU WILL NEED:

roasting pan (about 13" × 9 1/2")
measuring cups and spoons
large spoon (for basting)
serving platter

DIRECTIONS:

1. The turkey you choose for your Thanksgiving dinner will probably be frozen when it comes from the store. If so, it must be defrosted before you cook it. Just follow the directions on the package label. Be sure to read it in advance so you will have enough time—defrosting can take days.

2. After the turkey has been defrosted, remove the package of giblets and freeze. Put the turkey into the kitchen sink and run cold water over it. Remove any bits or pieces of turkey that may still be inside. Discard them.

3. Pat the turkey with the paper towels until it is dry and put it into the roasting pan.

4. Arrange the peeled and sliced carrots and onions around the turkey. Add the tomato sauce and then the water. Stir.

5. Sprinkle salt and garlic powder on the turkey and then pour the lemon juice over it.

6. Turn the oven on to 450° (ask an adult for help). Allow it to heat up—about 15 minutes—and then put the turkey in.

7. Turn the oven temperature down to 350°. After the turkey has been cooking for half an hour, baste it with the pan drippings. Every half hour baste the turkey, and if the gravy is beginning to cook down, add some more water.

Cook about 20 minutes for every pound of turkey.

8. When the turkey is almost cooked, with just about half an hour to go, spread the apricot jam on it. This will put a lovely glaze on your Thanksgiving turkey.

Cranberry and Ginger Ale Punch

This is very pretty looking and it's fun to drink!

INGREDIENTS YOU WILL NEED:

1 quart, 14 oz. cranberry juice
2 liters ginger ale
1 lemon washed and cut into 8 slices
8 cherries
8 toothpicks
ice cubes

UTENSILS YOU WILL NEED:

knife (to cut lemon slices)
large punch bowl

DIRECTIONS:

Prepare just before serving so the soda won't go flat.

1. Place a cherry in the center of each lemon slice using a toothpick to hold it in place.

2. In the large punch bowl, combine the cranberry juice and the ginger ale. Add the ice. Decorate with lemon-and-cherry slices.

Stuffing with Raisins

An almost effortless way to make delicious stuffing! Buy a bag of prepared stuffing and just add a few ingredients to it.

INGREDIENTS YOU WILL NEED:

1 large bag of stuffing mix
1 egg, beaten
1 cup chopped celery
1/2 cup vegetable oil
1 cup raisins (seedless)
1 cup orange juice
2 tablespoons vegetable oil

UTENSILS YOU WILL NEED:

9″ square baking dish
mixing bowl
spatula
measuring cups and spoons
aluminum foil

DIRECTIONS:

1. Turn the oven on to 350°. (Ask an adult for help.)
2. Combine all of the ingredients except vegetable oil in the mixing bowl.
3. Grease the baking dish with the 2 tablespoons of vegetable oil. Put the mixture into the baking dish and the dish into the oven.
4. Bake for 1/2 hour.
5. Turn the oven down to 200° to keep the stuffing warm. Cover loosely with aluminum foil. The turkey and potatoes can also be kept warm in this way. But don't do it for too long, or everything will dry out. Just long enough to get everything to the table at the same time!

Molasses Bread

This delicious quick bread comes from an old New England recipe. And to prove that two are better than one, the recipe makes two loaves!

INGREDIENTS YOU WILL NEED:

2 cups whole-wheat flour
1/2 cup sifted all-purpose flour
2 teaspoons baking soda
1 teaspoon salt
2 cups milk
1/2 cup molasses
1/2 teaspoon cinnamon
1 cup seedless raisins
2 tablespoons vegetable oil

UTENSILS YOU WILL NEED:

large mixing bowl
spatula
measuring cups and spoons
2 loaf pans (8 1/2″ × 4 1/2″ × 2 5/8″)
toothpick

DIRECTIONS:

1. Use 1 tablespoon vegetable oil to grease each of the loaf pans.
2. Combine all the other ingredients in the large mixing bowl and stir well.
3. Divide the mixture in half and put into the loaf pans. Let stand 1/2 hour.
4. Turn the oven to 350° (Ask an adult for help.) Bake for 45—50 minutes or until a toothpick inserted into the center of the loaf comes out clean.
5. Carefully run a knife around the loaves to loosen them from the pans. After the loaves have cooled off, turn them out of the pans.

Sweet Potatoes with Peaches

These smell wonderful as they are cooking.

INGREDIENTS YOU WILL NEED:

2 large cans sweet potatoes
1 medium-sized can of sliced peaches (used
    with the liquid)
1/2 teaspoon cinnamon
3/4 cup brown sugar

UTENSILS YOU WILL NEED:

13″ × 9 1/2″ baking dish
measuring cups and spoons
mixing spoon

DIRECTIONS:

1. Open cans of sweet potatoes and peaches.
Arrange in the baking dish. Add the liquid from
the peaches.
2. Sprinkle the cinnamon and brown sugar
over the mixture.
3. Turn the oven to 350°. (Ask an adult for
help.) Bake for 20 minutes. Stir the mixture and
continue baking for 15—25 minutes more until
there is a coating over the potatoes.

18

Fresh Cranberry Sauce with Oranges

As you are making this dish you will notice what a wonderful color the cranberries are. In colonial days they were used to dye yarn and cloth.

INGREDIENTS YOU WILL NEED:

1 pound package fresh cranberries
2 cups sugar
2 cups water
1/4 cup orange juice
large orange (peeled and cut into small pieces)

UTENSILS YOU WILL NEED:

medium-sized saucepan
medium-sized bowl
measuring cups and spoons

DIRECTIONS:

1. Wash the cranberries and throw away any that are crushed or spoiled.
2. Put the sugar and water in the saucepan and stir until they have been combined. Then bring the mixture to a boil. Be careful not to let it boil over—use low heat and move pan from heat as soon as it bubbles.
3. Add the cranberries, orange juice, and orange.
4. Simmer mixture on low heat for about 5—10 minutes, or until the berries become soft. Skim off any foam from the top of the mixture. Cool.
5. Pour into a bowl and put into the refrigerator for several hours.

English Trifle

Just assemble the ingredients and put them in a fancy bowl and this yummy dessert is ready to serve. This is an old-time British favorite that was brought to America in colonial times.

INGREDIENTS YOU WILL NEED:

1/2 package ladyfingers, or other spongelike cookie. Cut each ladyfinger in half.

1 package instant lemon pudding, prepared according to package instructions

1 package frozen strawberries, defrosted.

1 cup sliced canned pears

1 large container prepared whipped cream

UTENSILS YOU WILL NEED:

1 quart-size glass bowl. (Glass is the best because you can see all the layers of food.)
large mixing spoon

DIRECTIONS:

1. Line the bottom of the bowl with cookies or ladyfingers.
2. Now spread some lemon pudding, then some strawberries, then whipped cream and finally all of the pears.
3. Repeat a layer of ladyfingers, lemon pudding, strawberries and finish with the whipped cream.

Butter Cookies

These won't last long so don't put them on the table until everyone has finished the main course.

INGREDIENTS YOU WILL NEED:

3/4 cup sifted all-purpose flour
1/2 cup butter (softened)
1/2 teaspoon vanilla
1/2 cup confectioner's sugar

UTENSILS YOU WILL NEED:

mixing bowl
electric or hand beater
measuring cups and spoons
spatula
large tablespoon (for putting cookies onto
    cookie sheets)
2 cookie sheets

DIRECTIONS:

1. Turn the oven on to 350° (ask an adult for help.)
2. Combine the butter and the vanilla. Beat until light and fluffy.
3. Gradually add the sugar and the flour. Beat until smooth.
4. Spoon the mixture onto the cookie sheets in little mounds about 1″ apart.
5. Bake the cookies until they are golden brown along the edges. This should take about 15 minutes.

   Yield: 3 dozen cookies.

Mayflower Thanksgiving Dinner Invitation

Here's an antique-looking invitation to give to grandparents or friends to come and join you for a Thanksgiving feast. Making it look old by dipping it into coffee or tea makes it even more fun.

MATERIALS:

8 1/2″ × 11″ piece of white paper
1/4 cup instant coffee or 3 tea bags
wax paper
tracing paper
carbon paper
pencil
black fine line felt tip marker
6″ piece of ribbon

Dear Grandma and Grandpa,
Please come to our special Thanksgiving dinner at 4 o'clock.
love,
Oliver

METHOD:

1. Fill the kitchen sink with about 2″ of warm water. Add 1/4 cup instant coffee or three tea bags.

2. Carefully place the paper in the sink and soak. The paper becomes very delicate when it is wet, so try not to move it around too much or it will tear. The paper will wrinkle, which is part of the antique look.

3. Leave the paper in the coffee or tea solution for about 3 minutes or until it is a little darker than the color you want. The paper will dry a lighter color than it looks when it is wet.

4. Holding the paper at the corners, lightly and carefully shake off the excess liquid. Place the antiqued paper on a piece of wax paper and allow it to dry.

5. Now trace the design for the ship onto the tracing paper.

6. Place the carbon paper on top of your invitation and then put the traced design over the carbon paper. Draw over the design with a pencil, making sure to press firmly and evenly. When you lift off the tracing and carbon papers you will have a copy of the design on the antiqued paper.

7. Now go over the outlines of the design with the black felt tip marker.

8. Underneath your drawing write "Please come to our house for a special Thanksgiving dinner," give the time to arrive, and sign the card.

24

Gobble, Gobble Turkey Centerpiece

This three-dimensional turkey will sit contentedly on your Thanksgiving table ready to receive your guests. He is a delight to make and quickly comes alive from pieces of colored oaktag.

MATERIALS:

rectangle of orange oaktag, 4″ × 14 3/4″ (for body)
circle of orange oaktag, 5 1/4″ across (for chest)
cardboard tube from bathroom tissue, 4 1/2″ long, (for neck)
two 1″ circles of white paper (for eyes)
6″ square of green felt and 24″ of yellow rickrack (for decorative covering)
22″ × 28″ piece of newspaper to stuff the body of the turkey
yellow poster paint
1/4″ paint brush
white glue
tracing paper, pencil
scissors
stapler
black felt tip marker
brown paper—use paper bag
small piece red felt
small piece yellow oaktag
orange oaktag
cardboard for nose

METHOD:

1. Take the rectangle of orange oaktag and staple the ends together with three staples, overlapping the edges about one inch. You should now have a circle of oaktag about 5″ across that will form the turkey's body.

2. Crumble the piece of newspaper up and use it to stuff the opening of the oaktag circle.

3. Glue the 5 1/4″ circle of orange oaktag (turkey's chest piece) to one side of the open circle, as shown.

25

4. Now make all the patterns that you will need to complete the different parts of the turkey. Transfer the patterns to the following materials:

eyes: white paper (make two)
wings: brown paper (make two)
nose: cardboard
gizzard: red felt
medium tailfeather: yellow oaktag
large tailfeather: orange oaktag

5. Cut out all parts. Pattern for medium tailfeather is shown inside of pattern for large tailfeather.

6. Glue the medium tailfeather to the turkey and the large tailfeather to the medium tailfeather, as shown. Glue one wing on each side of the turkey's body.

7. To make the turkey's head and neck, take the 4 1/2" tube and paint it with yellow poster paint. Let it dry thoroughly. Then glue the nose into place, checking the illustration for proper placement.

8. To make the turkey's eyes, draw a black circle with a felt tip marker on each of the white circles, as shown.

9. Take the gizzard of red felt, fold, and glue into place as shown.

10. Now glue the completed head and neck in place, as shown, and hold it for a few minutes until it begins to dry. Let the turkey rest on its tailfeathers for about 15 minutes until it is thoroughly dry.

11. For the turkey's blanket, cut the 24" piece of rickrack into four 6" pieces. Glue each piece along the outside edge of the square of green felt. The rickrack can overlap slightly at the corners. Use only a little bit of glue and try not to let it run.

Mr. Turkey is now ready to display proudly on your Thanksgiving table!

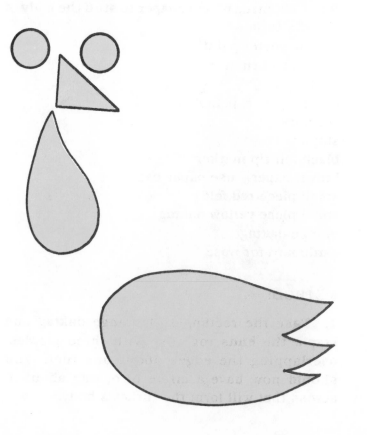

Tom Turkey Table Toppers

These fun placemats will liven up your Thanksgiving table settings. Three main designs are given: Tom Turkey, a house, and a tree. In addition to the main design, each placemat has another design for the corners—you can choose either a star or a flower.

MATERIALS:

12″ × 16″ piece of unbleached muslin for each placemat
pencil, tracing paper, carbon paper
black permanent felt tip marker
colored crayons
brown wrapping paper, newspaper
an iron and ironing board

METHOD:

1.   Trace the patterns of your choice onto the tracing paper and then transfer them onto the unbleached muslin, using carbon paper (see the directions on page 23). You will need a main design, and small designs for the corners.

2.   Make the outlines of your designs permanent by going over the carbon lines with a black permanent felt tip marker. Make sure you protect your table or work surface by laying down newspaper first, in case the marker bleeds through the cloth.

3.   Crayon in the design in colors you like. Some suggestions: the turkey could be in brown, yellow, and orange, the house in red and brown, the tree in brown and green, the stars red, and the flowers yellow.

4.   Place the finished mat crayoned side up on an ironing board and put a piece of brown wrap-

ping paper on top. Gently iron to set the color and make it shiny.

29

31

32

Autumn Leaves

Many autumn leaves turn color—bright yellow, orange, red, rust. . . . Collect samples from the many varieties of trees. You can make some unusual pictures with the more interesting leaves by adding a few details with a felt tip marker.

MATERIALS:

leaves
white paper (for background)
felt tip markers in several colors (including
    black)
heavy book
paper towels

METHOD:

1. Collect some pretty leaves that you would enjoy working with. Try to collect leaves of different shapes. Then place them between two paper towels and press them under a heavy book. Leave them for two or three days to flatten and dry.

2. Now take a leaf and glue it to a piece of white paper. Use the felt tip markers to draw a head, face, arms, and legs. Check the illustrations for some ideas for your leaf pictures.

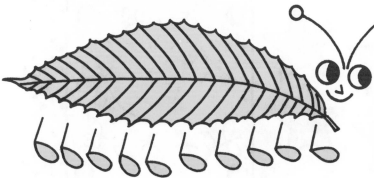

Wilson and Wilhelmina Mouse

Wilson and Wilhelmina Mouse settle in under their warm patchwork quilt for a long nap. They have just finished dining on their Thanksgiving feast of tasty leftover crumbs. This easy-to-make fabric picture can be framed and hung up in your room or given to a special friend.

MATERIALS:

white oaktag, 6″ × 8″ and 8″ × 10″
printed fabric (calico), 8″ × 10″
strip of fabric, 3/8″ × 2″
scraps of colored and printed fabric
9 cotton balls
8″ piece of ribbon
white thread
pencil, ruler, scissors
tracing paper, carbon paper
tape, white glue
grey and pink colored pencils
black fine line felt tip marker

METHOD:

Mice

1. Trace the design for the mice onto tracing paper.
2. Place the carbon paper over the 6″ × 8″ piece of oaktag. Now put the traced design over the carbon paper, checking the illustration for proper placement. Gently tape the two sheets down on the oaktag. This will prevent the papers from sliding around. Draw over the design again with a pencil, making sure to press firmly and evenly. When you lift off the tracing and carbon papers you will have a copy of the mice design on the white oaktag.

3. Now go over the outlines with a black felt tip marker. Color the mice grey with black eyes and pink noses.
4. Trace the pattern for the mouse arms. Make two—one arm for each mouse. Transfer the pattern onto the oaktag and cut out. Color with grey pencil and put them aside until later. After the quilt has been glued onto the oaktag the arms will be glued on top of it.

Quilt

1. Cut out nine 2″ square pieces of fabric from scraps of colored printed fabric.

35

2. Glue a cotton ball to the reverse side of each square. This will give the quilt a puffy effect. Be sure to use only a tiny bit of glue so it doesn't run and make the square messy.

3. To cover the mice with their quilt: Start at the upper left hand edge (see illustration) and glue each of the squares into place by applying a small amount of glue along the reverse of the outside edges. Each row has three squares. Finish the top row and then do the middle and bottom rows, working from left to right. Be sure to work neatly so that the rows of squares are glued close together to look like a real quilt.

4. Glue the arms into place on top of the quilt, checking the illustration for proper placement.

5. To make Wilhelmina's bow, take the 3/8″ × 2″ strip of fabric and glue the ends together.

Pinch the bow at the center and wind a 4″ piece of thread around the center of the bow. Glue into place as shown.

6. Cut out a small heart from a piece of fabric and glue into place. As a final touch you can draw "bubbles" above the mice and write in a message.

Frame

1. Glue the 8″ × 10″ piece of fabric to the 8″ × 10″ piece of oaktag. Spread a small amount of glue along the outside edges. Now center the finished picture on the frame and glue it down.

2. To hang your picture, glue the ends of a ribbon to each side of the top edge. Put a small piece of tape over the glued ends and allow to dry thoroughly.

Sylvan Squirrel

Squirrels are great collectors, at this time of year squirrels are busy collecting acorns to bury in the ground and eat later. You can make this friendly squirrel and he will collect your messages for you! Just hang him on the door of your room and people can leave their messages with him.

MATERIALS:

2 squares grey felt for squirrel
1 square white felt for inside of tail and envelope
scrap of black felt for eyes and nose
3, 1″ pieces of black yarn for whiskers
24″ piece of black yarn to hang squirrel from
tracing paper, pencil
needle, straight pins
scissors, glue, polyester batting
1″ × 2″ piece of white paper for envelope
black felt tip marker

METHOD:

1. Make a pattern for the squirrel and the inside of his tail, by tracing the designs given.
2. Place the two squares of grey felt on top of each other. Place the pattern for the squirrel on top of them and trace around the outline with a pencil. Remove the pattern and pin the two pieces of felt together so they hold steady. Cut the pattern on the line that you have just drawn, leaving the pins in.
3. Cut out the pattern for the inside of the tail from the white felt.
4. From the scrap of black felt cut out an eye and a nose. Checking the illustration, glue the eye and nose into place. Then glue the three 1″ long whiskers into place. Now glue the inside of the tail into place to complete the squirrel.
5. Sew around the outside edge of the squirrel with the grey thread, leaving the pins in. Leave a 1 1/2″ opening for the stuffing to go through.

6. Now stuff the squirrel, and when you have finished stitch up the opening.
7. To make the envelope that will hold the messages, first cut a 4″ square from the white felt. Fold it in half so that you have a 2″ × 4″ rectangle. Put glue along the 2″ sides to make the envelope. The message fits into the top of the envelope. On the 1″ × 2″ piece of paper write the word "message" with the black felt tip marker and glue into place. Checking the illustration, glue the envelope onto the squirrel.
8. Take the 24″ piece of black yarn and knot one end and sew the other end to the squirrel as shown. Now Sylvan Squirrel is ready to go to work for you!

40

Pilgrim and Native American Paper Puppets

These paper cutouts are dressed in authentic costumes. This is how people looked at the first Thanksgiving dinner. You can make them walk by putting your index and middle fingers into the rings on the back of each figure. Then they can stroll off to the first Thanksgiving feast.

MATERIALS:

white oaktag
tracing paper
pencil, colored pencils, felt tip markers
scissors
masking tape, glue

METHOD:

1. Make patterns for the figures by tracing the designs given and cutting the tracing paper along the outlines.
2. Place the patterns on the oaktag and cut out.
3. Checking the illustration, draw in the details of the figure you have chosen to make. Use a pencil at first, and when you are satisfied with what you have drawn, go over the pencil line with a felt tip marker.
4. Color the figure with either pencils or felt tip markers. Use grey, brown, beige, black, and navy for the pilgrims and brighter colors for the Indians.
5. To make the figures stand, you will have to make tabs of oaktag 1/2" wide by 3" long. One tab is needed for each figure. Curve the tab around your finger and tape the ends together to form a small ring that your finger can fit through. Now glue one ring to the back of each figure. Place a finger in the ring.

41

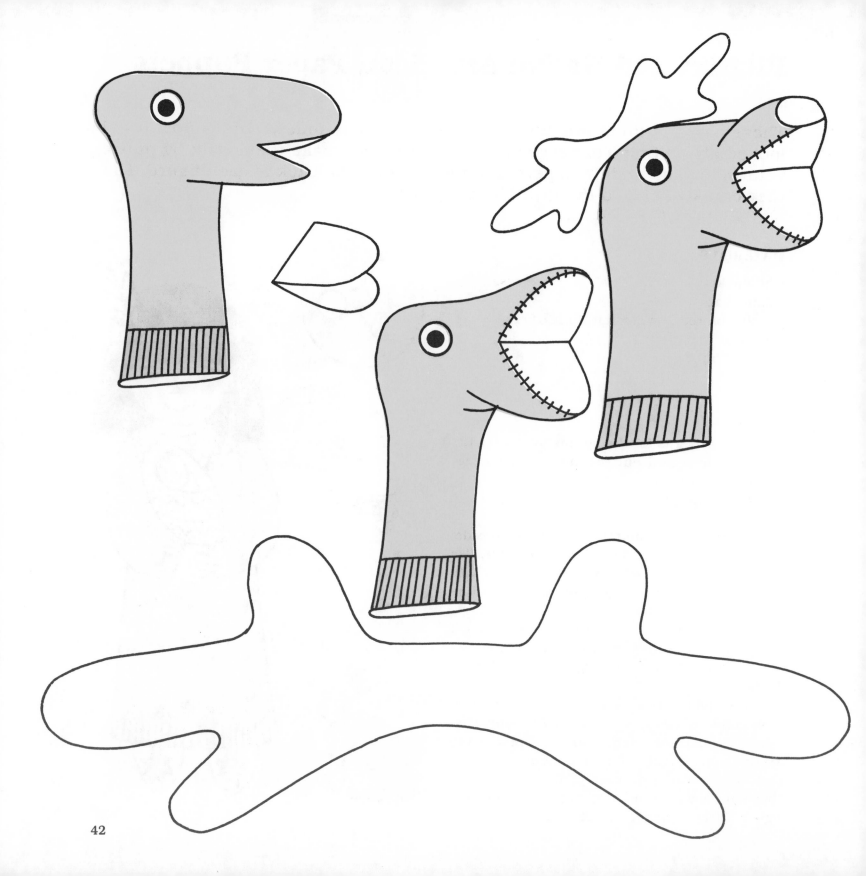

42

Michael Moose Puppet

One-two-three and Michael the Moose puppet is made! Use one of your father's old socks or any other large sock.

MATERIALS:

large sock, preferably brown or black
cardboard, 4" × 8"
tracing paper
squares of felt in red, yellow, white, pink, and
    black
scissors
dark thread, yellow thread
needle
tape
two black buttons
cotton batting

METHOD:

1. Cut a slit in the toe of the sock. (Look at the illustration).
2. Now fold the cardboard in half widthwise. Trim it to fit into the slit of the sock.
3. Cut red felt to cover the inside of the cardboard. The felt should extend 1/4" beyond the cardboard on each end.
4. Fit the felt-covered cardboard into the sock. Sew the extra flaps of felt to the inside of the slit, as shown. You now have the moose's mouth.
5. For the eyes, cut two 1" circles from the white felt. Glue a black button onto each white circle.
6. To make Michael Moose's antlers, cut a tracing paper pattern. Pin the pattern to the yellow felt, which has been folded in half. Cut the felt along the pattern. Using yellow thread, sew the two halves together along the edges—leave a 2" opening at the bottom of the antlers for stuffing. Stuff the antlers with cotton batting and then sew up the opening. Glue the antlers into place, checking the illustration.
7. From a scrap of red or pink felt cut out a small circle for a nose and glue it into place.

Put your hand inside the moose and you will have a fun puppet to entertain you and your friends and family.

Native American Soap Charm

Native Americans believed that animal charms brought good luck, if they were well treated. Carve your animal charms out of large bars of white soap, attach an arrowhead, and put a food offering out for them. An acorn, pea, or kernel of corn is all you need.

Designs are given for a bear and a fish.

MATERIALS:

large bar of white soap
pencil, knife
tracing paper
scissors, tape
turquoise felt tip marker
white oaktag
colored yarn or string

METHOD: -

1. Trace the design for the bear and the fish onto the tracing paper.
2. Tape the drawing onto the bar of soap, as shown.
3. Draw over the design firmly with a pencil and remove the tracing paper. Check to see if all of the design has gone onto the soap. If not, go over it again with the pencil.
4. Begin carving away large sections of the soap until you have the rough shape of the animal. Then you can carefully carve the outline until you are satisfied. Indian carvings didn't have much detail so yours don't need them either. The fish scales and the bear fur can be etched in quickly with a knife. Remember to carve out eyes and give your animals a smile!

5. Draw the outline of the arrowhead on the oaktag and cut it out. Color it with the turquoise marker. Tie it onto the animal with yarn, as shown. Now feed your animal—and good luck!

45

"Deerskin" Story Cloth

At the time of the Pilgrims, the Indian tribes of North America did not have a written language such as we use today. They used hand signs and drew pictures to communicate words and ideas. The Indians measured the years in "moons," and the moon is one of their most popular signs.

Henry Wadsworth Longfellow's famous poem "The Song of Hiawatha" mentions some of these symbols:

"For the earth he drew a straight line,

For the sky a bow above it;

White the space between for daytime,

Filled with little stars for night-time;

On the left a point for sunrise,

On the right a point for sunset,

On the top a point for noontide,

And for rain and cloudy weather

Waving lines descending from it."

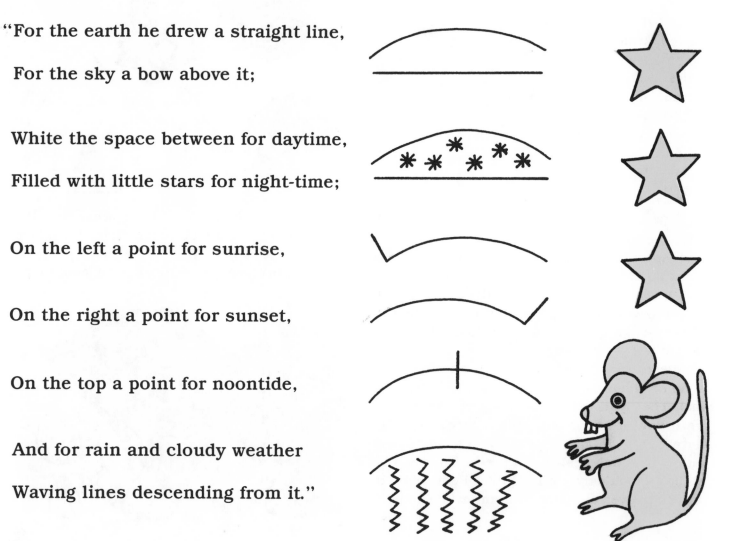

Use your imagination to make up your own sign language. Then use the language you have created to tell a story for presentation at Thanksgiving dinner. The story can be about a funny or exciting thing that has happened to you. Or you can tell the guests about all the things for which everyone should be especially thankful!

MATERIALS:

muslin, an old sheet, or brown wrapping paper
scissors
felt tip markers in assorted bright colors

METHOD:

1. Cut a "deerskin" from the material you have chosen, using the outline shown in the illustration. With a felt tip marker, draw in your story on the "skin" using the symbols shown in the illustration and/or other symbols you have made up yourself. Then add color as you wish.

2. To store and transport your finished story "skin", just roll it up and tie it with a piece of black ribbon or scrap of muslin.

Calendar

At Thanksgiving time the year is almost over, and it is a good time to make a calendar ready for the coming year. Here are 12 designs to use on your calendar plus some interesting facts about the months of the year that can be written underneath the drawings.

MATERIALS:

12 sheets of white paper, 8 1/2″ × 11″
tracing paper
carbon paper
black, fine line felt tip marker, pencil
colored markers
ruler
12″ piece of colored yarn
hole punch, stapler
calendar to use as a model

METHOD:

1. Trace the design for each month onto the tracing paper.
2. Place the carbon paper over a sheet of white paper. Now put the traced design over the carbon paper, checking the illustration for proper placement. Draw over the design with a pencil, making sure to press evenly and firmly. When you lift off the tracing and carbon papers you will have a copy of the design on the white paper. Go over the outlines with a black felt tip marker. Color in the designs as you like.
3. Checking a calendar, draw in the dates beneath each of your drawings for each month. Use a ruler to draw the lines. The name of each month should be written in large letters (see the illustration). Write in the days of the month, and highlight each month's holidays with a star.

4. Put the finished twelve sheets of paper in order of the months. Staple them together at the top edge—one staple at each end and one in the center. This way you can pull off each month as it is finished.
5. To hang your calendar, make a hole 1/4″ down and 1/4″ in from the top corner of each sheet with a hole punch. (See illustration.) Make sure the hole is in the same place on every sheet.

Put the yarn through the holes and tie each end in a knot.

January

January was named for the Roman god Janus. Janus could look into the future and also into the past, and January is our link with the old year and the new. The January flower is the carnation, and the birthstone is the garnet.

February

February comes from Februarius, the Latin word that means "to purify." The Ancient Romans purified themselves of their wrongdoings by penitence during this month. The February flower is the violet, and the birthstone is the amethyst.

March

March was named for the Roman month Martius that honored Mars, the god of war. The March flower is the daffodil, and the birthstone is the bloodstone. Spring begins this month.

April

April comes from the Latin word aperiere meaning "to open" (like a flower). The April flower is the sweet pea and the birthstone is the diamond.

May

May was named for Maia, the Roman goddess of "growth and increase." The May flower is the lily of the valley, and the birthstone is the emerald.

June

June was named for Juno, the Roman goddess of women. She was also the wife of Jupiter, the king of the gods. The June flower is the rose, and the birthstone is the pearl. Summer begins this month.

July

July was named for Julius Caesar. The July flower is the larkspur, and the birthstone is the ruby.

August

August was named for the Roman Emperor Augustus. The August flower is the gladiolus, and the birthstone is the sardonyx. There are no formal holidays to celebrate in August, so invent your own.

September

Septem, the Roman word for "seven," is what September comes from. In the old Roman calendar Septem was the seventh month. The September flower is the aster, and the birthstone is the sapphire. Autumn begins this month.

October

Octo, the Roman word for "eight," is what October is named for. In the old Roman calendar Octo was the eighth month. The October flower is the calendula, and the birthstone is the opal.

November

Novem, the Roman word for "nine," became November. In the old Roman calendar this was the ninth month. The November flower is the chrysanthemum, and the birthstone is the topaz.

December

Decem, the Roman word for "ten," gave December its name. In the old Roman calendar this was the tenth month. The December flower is the narcissus, and the birthstone is the turquoise. Winter begins this month.

Start a Mini Garden at Thanksgiving

The amaryllis and the paperwhite narcissus are fantastic flowers that grow from bulbs and will bloom indoors in midwinter. They are simple to grow and are specially prepared to flower fast. They are planted in the earth or water. Soon a stem shoots to the surface. After a while the stem develops leaves, and flowers begin to bud and then bloom. You will need to get the bulbs at your local gardening shop or from a mail-order gardening catalog.

You will be thankful to have fresh flowers growing in your house in winter—and it all started at Thanksgiving!

Amaryllis

The amaryllis is a spectacular flower that comes in white, red, pink, orange, and even stripes. Each bulb will produce a cluster of 3 or 4 giant flowers. Some flowers grow 5″ across and range in height from 12″ to 28″.

MATERIALS:

one amaryllis bulb
rich potting soil (like the kind used to plant African violets)
clay pot—twice the size of the bulb, with a drainage hole at the bottom
clay saucer that fits under the clay pot
pebbles

METHOD:

1. Place the saucer under the pot and then put 1″ of pebbles into the pot.
2. Now add enough potting soil to fill up half the pot.
3. Examine the amaryllis bulb, and you will notice that one end has some beginning roots and the other end has a small shoot. Make sure the *roots* are placed going toward the soil. Add enough soil to cover two-thirds of the bulb. Do not fill pot to the top—leave about an inch free of soil so that water will not overflow.
4. Water the bulb thoroughly so that all the soil is moist. The saucer underneath the pot will collect any excess water. From now on, only water your plant a little bit until the sprout begins to grow. Then gradually increase the amount of water you use and keep the plant moist.
5. Keep your plant out of direct sunlight and at room temperature. If you are keeping it on a windowsill be sure that it does not get any cold

drafts from windows or doors opening or it will freeze. Your plant will grow quickly—within four to six weeks the first flowers will appear.

Paperwhite narcissus

These are some of the simplest of bulbs to grow indoors. They are white, star-shaped flowers that smell wonderful. They take only about one month to bloom, so if you plant them at Thanksgiving you'll have them blooming at Christmas!

MATERIALS:

4 paperwhite narcissus bulbs
ceramic pot, 6″ across by 4″ high. This pot should *not* have a hole at the bottom, because you are going to grow these bulbs in a bed of pebbles and water
pebbles—enough to fill the pot

METHOD:

1.   Place a layer or bed of pebbles in a clean pot. The pebbles should be about 2″ high. Now place the bulbs on top of the pebbles, roots down. Leave about 1″ between each bulb so they have room to breathe and grow. Add more pebbles so that the bulbs are supported.
2.   Pour water into the pot until it just reaches the tops of the bulbs. From now on all you will have to do is to keep them watered this way. Your plants can be kept on a windowsill but should not have direct sunlight.

63

Index

About Thanksgiving, 10
Amaryllis, 61-62
Amethyst, 50
Animal charms, 45
April, 52
Aster, 57
August, 56
Autumn leaves, 33

Bear, 45
Birthstones, 48-60
Bloodstone, 51
Bread, 17

Calendar, 48-60
Calendula, 58
Carnation, 49
Centerpiece, 25-27
Chrysanthemum, 59
Cookies, 21
Cranberry sauce, 19

Daffodil, 51
December, 60
Deerskin story cloth, 46-47
Diamond, 52
Dinner invitation, 23
Dinner menu, 12

Emerald, 53
English trifle, 20

February, 50
Fish, 45
Flowers, 48-60, 61-63

Gardens, 61-63
Garnet, 49
Gladiolus, 56

January, 49
June, 54

July, 55

Larkspur, 55
Lily of the valley, 53

March, 51
May, 53
Mayflower, 23
Mice, 35
Months of the year, 48-60
Moose, 43

Narcissus, 61, 63
Native American, 41-42, 45

October, 58
Opal, 58

Pearl, 54
Pilgrims, 10, 41, 46
Punch, 15
Puppets, 41-43

Quilt, 35-36

Recipes, 13-21
Rose, 54
Ruby, 55

Sapphire, 57
Sardonyx, 56
Stuffing, 16
Sweet pea, 52
Sweet potatoes, 18
Sylvan Squirrel, 38-39

Table toppers, 29-31
Topaz, 59
Turkey, 14, 25-26, 29
Turquoise, 60

Vegetables, 13
Violet, 50

Wilson and Wilhelmina Mouse, 35-37